W9-ANW-394

YOUR PASSPORT TO

GUATEMALA

by Nancy Dickmann

CONTENT CONSULTANT

Todd Little-Siebold
Professor of History and Latin American Studies,
College of the Atlantic, Maine

CAPSTONE PRESS
a capstone imprint

Capstone Captivate is published by Capstone Press, an imprint of Capstone.
1710 Roe Crest Drive
North Mankato, Minnesota 56003
www.capstonepub.com

Library of Congress Cataloging-in-Publication Data is available on the Library of Congress website.
ISBN: 978-1-4966-9550-5 (hardcover)
ISBN: 978-1-4966-9718-9 (paperback)
ISBN: 978-1-9771-5542-9 (eBook PDF)

Summary: What would it be like to live in Guatemala? How is Guatemalan culture unique? Explore the sights, traditions, and daily lives of people in Guatemala.

Image Credits
Alamy: Scott B. Rosen, 23; Capstone: Eric Gohl, 5; Getty Images: Ann Ronan Pictures/Print Collector, 8, Ian MacNicol/FIFA, 28, Sharpshooters/VW Pics/Universal Images Group, 19, Tony Barson/FilmMagic, 11; iStockphoto: Lucy Brown - loca4motion, 25, Rainer Soegtrop, 27; Shutterstock: Diego Grandi, 21, fboudrias, 13, Laura G. Robe, 15, Milosz Maslanka, 17, Ondrej Prosicky, 7, Rob Crandall, 16, ROSITO, 14, salmon-negro, 20, SL-Photography, Cover, WitR, 9

Design Elements
iStockphoto: Yevhenii Dubinko; Shutterstock: Flipser, Gil C, KASUE, MicroOne, pingebat

Editorial Credits
Editor: Clare Lewis; Designer: Juliette Peters;
Media Research: Tracy Cummins; Premedia: Laura Manthe

All internet sites appearing in back matter were available and accurate when this book was sent to press.

Printed and bound in the United States of America. PO3837

CONTENTS

CHAPTER ONE
WELCOME TO GUATEMALA! 4

CHAPTER TWO
HISTORY OF GUATEMALA 8

CHAPTER THREE
EXPLORE GUATEMALA 12

CHAPTER FOUR
DAILY LIFE 18

CHAPTER FIVE
HOLIDAYS AND CELEBRATIONS 24

CHAPTER SIX
SPORTS AND RECREATION 28

GLOSSARY 30
READ MORE 31
INTERNET SITES 31
INDEX 32

Words in **bold** are in the glossary.

CHAPTER ONE

WELCOME TO GUATEMALA!

The rain forest is hot and humid. Brightly colored birds fly through the trees. A crumbling **temple** rises above the treetops. This is the ancient site of Tikal in Guatemala. People called the Maya built it thousands of years ago. Today, people come from all over the world to visit it.

Guatemala is a small country in Central America. More than 17 million people live there. Many of them are Maya. They still speak Maya languages. Many other people are a mix of Maya and Spanish. Spanish soldiers arrived in the 1500s. They controlled Guatemala for many years. Their **descendants** still speak Spanish today.

MAP OF GUATEMALA

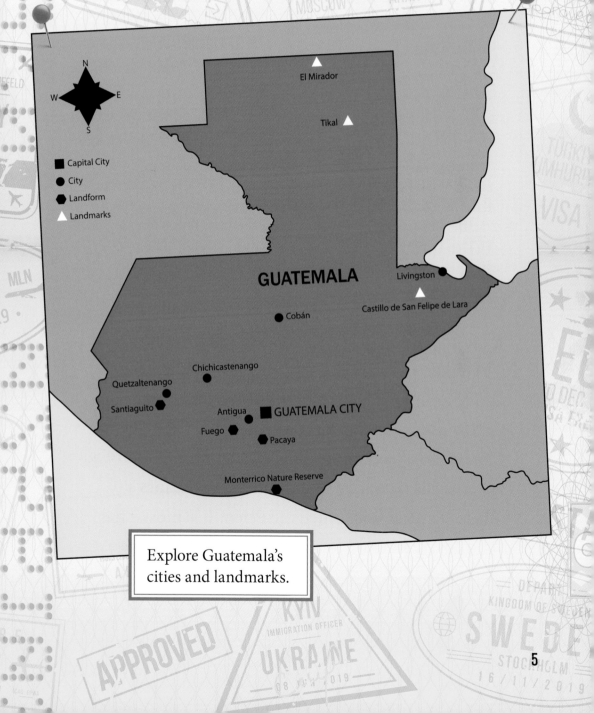

N
W E
S

El Mirador

Tikal

■ Capital City
● City
⬡ Landform
▲ Landmarks

GUATEMALA

Livingston

Castillo de San Felipe de Lara

Cobán

Chichicastenango

Quetzaltenango

Santiaguito

Antigua   ■ GUATEMALA CITY

Fuego

Pacaya

Monterrico Nature Reserve

Explore Guatemala's cities and landmarks.

FACT FILE

OFFICIAL NAME: ....REPUBLIC OF GUATEMALA
POPULATION: 17,889,773
LAND AREA: ....41,374 SQ. MI. (107,159 SQ KM)
CAPITAL: ....GUATEMALA CITY
MONEY: ....QUETZAL
GOVERNMENT: ....PRESIDENTIAL REPUBLIC
LANGUAGE: ....SPANISH AND MANY MAYA LANGUAGES

GEOGRAPHY: Guatemala borders Mexico to the north and west. El Salvador and Honduras are to the south, and Belize is to the northeast. Guatemala has a long coastline on the Pacific Ocean and a shorter one on the Caribbean Sea.

NATURAL RESOURCES: Guatemala has metals, rubber, and oil. It also grows sugarcane, bananas, and coffee.

THREE PARTS

The land in Guatemala is divided into three main parts. Along the Pacific coast, there is a flat plain. The land is good for farming. The middle of the country has mountains and valleys. In the north, there is a large area called the Petén. It is mostly flat and covered in rain forests. Many Maya ruins are found here.

Ancient Maya rulers used the quetzal's feathers to make headdresses.

NATIONAL BIRD

A bird called the quetzal lives in the rain forest. It has bright blue, green, and red feathers. Males have tail feathers up to 3 feet (1 meter) long! This bird is a symbol of Guatemala. The country's currency is named after it.

CHAPTER TWO

HISTORY OF GUATEMALA

Civilization in Guatemala began about 4,000 years ago. People started to farm the land and set up towns. They made pottery and created art. By about 800 **BCE**, there were many villages. They traded with each other and began to build larger buildings.

By about 200 **CE**, the Maya had built grand cities. They had temples, palaces, and large open squares. The Maya had **irrigation** systems for watering their crops. They had a complex system of writing. They wrote stories and history on paper made from tree bark and on huge stone tablets.

Maya writing used picturelike symbols called glyphs.

FACT

After about 900 CE, most Maya cities were abandoned. Historians aren't sure why this happened. It may have been because of war or a long drought.

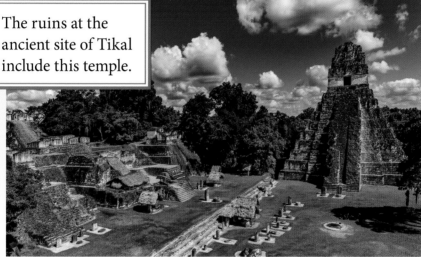

The ruins at the ancient site of Tikal include this temple.

THE SPANISH ARRIVE

The first Spanish soldiers arrived in Guatemala in 1524. They had guns and horses, which the Maya didn't. The Spanish soon took over. Many of the Maya were killed. Others died from disease. Many of them were forced to work for the Spanish.

TIMELINE OF GUATEMALAN HISTORY

ABOUT 2000 BCE: People start to farm and build settlements in Guatemala.

ABOUT 250 CE: The Maya begin to organize into city-states, each with its own king.

ABOUT 900 CE: Maya sites start to be abandoned.

1524: Spanish soldiers under the command of Pedro de Alvarado arrive in Guatemala.

1821: A group of *criollos* declare Guatemala to be independent.

1847: Guatemala becomes a republic.

1941: Guatemala enters World War II on the side of the Allies.

1960: A civil war begins between the government and the poor and indigenous populations.

1992: Rigoberta Menchú wins the Nobel Peace Prize for her fight for the rights of indigenous people in Guatemala.

1996: A ceasefire ends the civil war. Many Maya communities are left devastated.

INDEPENDENCE

The Spanish controlled Guatemala for nearly 300 years. But in the early 1800s, a group called *criollos* became more powerful. These people were descended from the Spanish. But they had been born in Guatemala. Many of them owned large areas of land. They wanted to rule themselves. They and other groups began to fight for their independence.

In 1821, Guatemala became **independent** from Spain. But the country's Maya were still not truly free. The criollos ruled over them.

CIVIL WAR

In the years after independence, Guatemala had many different rulers. In 1960, a terrible **civil war** began. Many poor people banded together to fight the government. They included many of the country's **indigenous** people. The war finally ended in 1996.

Rigoberta Menchú (1959–) is a human rights activist. She speaks out against the government's unfair treatment of the Maya.

CHAPTER THREE

EXPLORE GUATEMALA

Tourists come to Guatemala for its beautiful scenery. The country has mountains and lakes. There are also beautiful beaches. The dense rain forests are filled with wildlife. Tourists also come to see Maya culture and sites. They visit the country's modern cities too.

VOLCANOES

Guatemala has more than two dozen **volcanoes**. They stretch out in a line that runs from the Mexican border to the border with El Salvador. Many of the volcanoes are dormant. This means they haven't erupted for a long time. Others are extinct. They will probably never erupt. But three of them are still active! They are called Fuego, Santiaguito, and Pacaya.

FACT
|||||||||||||

The Fuego volcano had a
very large eruption in 2018.

BEACHES

Guatemala's beaches are among its secret treasures. Many of them are rarely crowded. Surfers enjoy the pounding waves. People take boats out to fish or to spot whales. The beach at Monterrico is part of a nature reserve. Sea turtles come here each year to lay eggs.

Baby turtles head to the sea soon after hatching in the sand.

FACT

The sand on some of Guatemala's beaches is black. It is made from cooled lava. Over many years, the pounding waves have turned it into sand.

BEAUTIFUL CITIES

Guatemala City is the country's largest city. It is a busy city with modern buildings. Most of the older buildings were destroyed in earthquakes in 1917 and 1918. Tourists often visit Antigua instead. This city was founded by the Spanish in 1543. There are cobbled streets and old churches.

Quetzaltenango is in the western part of the country. It is the largest city in the Maya region. Tourists also visit the smaller town of Chichicastenango. It has a huge open-air market. People sell fabric, pottery, and other Maya crafts.

Chichicastenango's market is one of the largest in Central America.

Tourists can climb Tikal's tallest pyramid, which appeared in the movie *Star Wars:* Episode IV-*A New Hope.*

ANCIENT SITES

Guatemala's Maya heritage attracts many tourists. They visit villages where Maya people still live today. They also visit the ancient sites built by these people's **ancestors**. Tikal is the most famous site. It has five steep pyramids built of stone. They served as temples. One of them is 212 feet (65 m) tall! Some visitors climb to the top. They can see other temples poking through the trees.

Tikal has thousands of other buildings. **Archaeologists** have discovered tombs and palaces. There are also courts where the Maya played a ball game. Teams tried to get a rubber ball through a hoop.

El Mirador is another stunning Maya site. It is even bigger than Tikal. But it is deep in the rain forest. Few tourists make it this far.

CASTILLO DE SAN FELIPE DE LARA

In about 1652, the Spanish built a fort along the Dulce River. It guarded the entrance to Lake Izabal. It was designed to keep pirates from looting the port along the lake's coast. However, pirates did capture the fort at least once. In later years, it was used as a prison.

CHAPTER FOUR

DAILY LIFE

About half of Guatemalans live in rural areas. Many of them live in the north of the country. They live in small villages and farm the land. Most of the people in the north are Maya. They often still wear traditional clothes. They speak over 20 different Maya languages. Their religion is a mix of Christian and Maya beliefs.

Life in the countryside is not always easy. There are few doctors. Children may have to travel a long way to school. Some of them work on farms instead of going to school. The average age for stopping school is 11.

Schools in the countryside are often small.

THE GARIFUNA

A group called the Garifuna live in Guatemala. Their ancestors were enslaved people from Africa. The enslaved people were taken from Africa to work in the Caribbean. They rebelled to try to free themselves and were sent away from the Caribbean. Many ended up settling in Guatemala.

FARMING

There are many farms in Guatemala. Volcanic **lava** has made the soil rich. It is very good for growing crops. People grow corn, beans, and other vegetables to eat. Farmers also grow crops to sell to other countries. They include coffee, sugar, bananas, and spices.

This indigenous woman is taking her crops to sell at a market.

CITY LIFE

About 3 million people live in Guatemala City. Many others live in smaller cities and towns. Life is different in the cities than it is in the countryside. There are shops, restaurants, and parks. There are traffic jams too!

Guatemalans are known for being friendly and laid-back. Family life is very important. Several generations of the same family will often live together. Many Guatemalans have moved to the United States to work. They send money to support their family back home.

This cathedral and busy square are in Guatemala City.

FOOD AND DRINK

Guatemalans enjoy sharing meals with family and friends. The food is a mix of Maya and Spanish traditions. There are African and Caribbean influences too. Many dishes are based on tortillas, corn, pork, chicken, and cheese. There are also tropical fruits, such as mangoes and avocados.

POPULAR DISHES

There are two classic dishes that are eaten across the country. One is chicken *pepián.* It is a spicy stew of chicken, fruit, and vegetables. It is served with rice and tortillas. The other meal is *kak'ik.* This is a turkey soup with chilis. The recipe goes back to Maya times.

For a quick snack, many people eat empanadas. These crispy pastries are often filled with potato and spinach. They are often served with guacamole.

Guatemala is famous for its coffee.

HOT CHOCOLATE

Guatemala is sometimes called "the birthplace of chocolate." To the Maya, it was the food of the gods. It was traditionally served as a drink and it still is today.

Ingredients:
- hot cocoa bars
- milk
- cinnamon stick (or ground cinnamon)

Instructions:

1. For each serving, you will need 1–2 squares of cocoa and 1 cup of milk. One cinnamon stick is enough for two servings.
2. Put the chocolate, milk, and cinnamon into a saucepan.
3. Ask an adult to help you heat it gently, stirring occasionally, until the chocolate is dissolved.
4. Remove the cinnamon stick and whisk the chocolate to make it frothy.
5. Serve while still hot.

CHAPTER FIVE

HOLIDAYS AND CELEBRATIONS

Most people in Guatemala are Christian. This means that Christian festivals are very important. The week before Easter is Holy Week. People march through the streets carrying religious statues. In Antigua, people make colorful patterns on the streets. These pictures are called *alfombras.* They are made from colored sawdust.

Christmas celebrations start on December 7. People set fire to little piñatas that represent the devil. In the nine days before Christmas, they celebrate *Las Posadas.* Every night there is a procession. People carry lanterns and statues of Joseph and Mary.

In some villages, people make giant kites to celebrate the Day of the Dead.

DAY OF THE DEAD

On November 1 and 2, Guatemalans remember loved ones who have died. It is called the Day of the Dead. People visit graves and say prayers. There is music and dancing. It is a sad time, but a happy one too.

INDEPENDENCE DAY

The whole country celebrates on September 15. This is the day that Guatemala won its independence from Spain. People fly the Guatemalan blue and white flag and dress in those colors too. There are fireworks and parades with marching bands. Runners carry torches from village to village.

FOLK FESTIVALS

The city of Cobán hosts a folklore festival every summer. There are parades and exhibits of traditional art. There is Maya music and dancing. Girls wear Maya clothes to compete in a beauty pageant. The winner is crowned "Maya princess."

The famous *Palo Volador* is performed at several festivals. Its name means *flying pole*. Two dancers climb to the top of a tall pole. Then they jump off. Held by ropes, they hold poses and spin gradually to the ground. This ritual has been performed since Maya times.

The Palo Volador may have originally begun as a way to ask the gods to end a drought.

CHAPTER SIX

SPORTS AND RECREATION

Soccer is the most popular sport in Guatemala. People support the Guatemalan national team. The team hopes to qualify for a World Cup tournament soon. They have won other competitions.

Futsal is also popular in Guatemala. This is a type of soccer played on a hard court, usually indoors. There are five players on each team. Many people play for fun. The national team is also very successful.

Many of today's top professional soccer players got their start playing futsal.

OTHER SPORTS

Many people in Guatemala play baseball. Kayaking is also popular. There are volcanoes to climb and caves to explore. There is something for everyone in Guatemala!

CINCOS

Cincos is a simple marble game played by children in Guatemala. You need two or more players, an area of dirt to play on, and a bunch of marbles shared equally.

1. Draw a triangle in the dirt. Each player puts one of their marbles inside.
2. Players take turns tossing or flicking a marble into the triangle, trying to knock one of the other players' marbles out.
3. If you knock someone's marble out, you get to keep it. If the marble that you used to knock it out stays inside the triangle, you get another turn.
4. If you don't hit anyone's marble, the marble that you tossed stays inside the triangle. You can pick it up on your next turn if no one has knocked it out by then.
5. The game ends when all the marbles are knocked out of the triangle. The player with the most marbles wins.

GLOSSARY

ancestor (AN-ses-tur)
a person from whom
someone is descended,
many generations ago

**archaeologist
(are-kee-OL-uh-jist)**
a person who studies
human history by
digging historic sites and
finding things

BCE/CE
BCE means Before
Common Era, or before
year one. CE means
Common Era, or after
year one

civil war (SIV-ul WAR)
a war fought between
different groups within
a country, rather than
between different countries

**descendant
(di-SEN-duhnt)**
originally coming
from a certain group,
generations ago

**independent
(in-de-PEN-duhnt)**
not ruled over by
anyone else

**indigenous
(in-DI-jen-us)**
native to a place

**irrigation
(EAR-i-GAY-shun)**
a way of supplying water to
land to help crops grow

lava (LA-vuh)
hot, molten rock that
comes out of a volcano
when it erupts

temple (TEM-pul)
a sacred building where
religious rituals take place

volcano (vol-KAY-no)
a mountain with a crater
at the top, through which
lava, gas, and ash can erupt

READ MORE

Howell, Izzi. *The Genius of the Maya: Innovations from Past Civilizations*. New York: Crabtree Publishing Company, 2019.

Mattern, Joanne. *Guatemala*. Egremont, MA: Red Chair Press, 2019.

Rudolph, Jessica. *Guatemala*. New York: Bearport Publishing, 2016.

INTERNET SITES

Encyclopedia Britannica: Guatemala Fast Facts
britannica.com/place/Guatemala

National Geographic Kids: Guatemala Facts
kids.nationalgeographic.com/explore/countries/guatemala/

Travel from Home: Guatemala
visitguatemala.com/?lang=en

INDEX

beaches, 12, 14

Day of the Dead, 25

drink, 22, 23

earthquakes, 15
El Mirador, 17

farming, 6, 8, 18, 20
food, 22

Guatemala City, 5, 6, 15, 21

holidays, 24, 26

independence, 10–11, 26

Maya
culture, 12, 15, 16, 26
languages, 4, 6, 18
people, 4, 7, 8, 9, 10, 16, 18
ruins, 6, 9, 16–17
Menchú, Rigoberta, 11

quetzal, 7
Quetzaltenango, 15

rain forests, 4, 6, 7, 12, 17

school, 18, 19
Spanish settlers, 4, 9, 10
sports, 28–29

temples, 4, 8, 9
Tikal, 4, 9, 16–17

volcanoes, 12, 13

OTHER BOOKS IN THIS SERIES